IF A STORM

ANHINGA PRESS

For Matthew,
So glad to meet you here at
Sewanee and with many, many
thanks!
All best,

IF A STORM

ANNA ROSS

8/2/14

2012 ROBERT DANA-ANHINGA
PRIZE FOR POETRY

Selected by
Julianna Baggott

ANHINGA PRESS
TALLAHASSEE, FLORIDA 2013

Cover art: Ita Quilligan
Author photograph: Sierra Rothberg
Cover and text design: Carol Lynne Knight
Type Styles: titles set in Trajan Pro Bold and text set in Minion Pro

Library of Congress Cataloging-in-Publication Data
If a Storm by Anna Ross, First Edition
ISBN – 978-1-934695-33-3
Library of Congress Cataloging Card Number – 2013947722

Anhinga Press Inc. is a non-profit corporation
dedicated wholly to the publication and appreciation
of fine poetry and other literary genres.

For personal orders, catalogs
and information write to:
Anhinga Press
P.O. Box 3665
Tallahassee, Florida 32315
Website: www.anhinga.org
Email: info@anhinga.org

Published in the United States
by Anhinga Press
Tallahassee, Florida
First Edition, 2013

*for Andy
and for Ita and Charlie*

CONTENTS

ACKNOWLEDGMENTS

Grateful acknowledgment is made to the editors of the following publications, in which versions of the following poems first appeared:

AGNI Online: "Dear Flood"
Barrow Street: "Dear Hurricane"
Center: "Flight"
Dogwood: "Fuse"
GSU Review and *Hacks: 10 Years on Grub Street:* "Evidence"
The Best of Kore Press, 2012: "Balance," "Dear Flood,"
    and "Pray, Montana"
Memorious: "Miscarriage" and "What It Was Like"
The New Republic: "The Wasps"
The Paris Review: "Vineyard"
The Pinch: "Winter Feeding"
Perihelion: "Evening Aubade"
Rattapallax: "Under the Southern Cross"
Southern Poetry Review: "A Quickening"
Salamander: "What Her Mother Said"
Y.A.R.N.: "Evening Song"

The following poems were published in the chapbook *Hawk Weather,* winner of the 2008 New Women's Voices Prize in Poetry from Finishing Line Press and the 2009 Jean Pedrick Chapbook Award from the New England Poetry Club.

"Evidence," "Plague Column, Brno," "Vineyard," "A Natural History," "Evening Aubade," "Under the Southern Cross," "By Morning," "After the Badger," "Pray, Montana," "Hawk Weather," "Balance," "Miscarriage," "Out of Ether," "Wolf Tree," "Luna Moth," "Waiting Room," "The Sea Wall," and "Flight."

Many thanks to Grub Street, the Massachusetts Cultural Council, the Sewanee Writers' Conference, and the Colrain Conferences for fellowships and support during the writing of this book, and to my many teachers, including Lucie Brock-Broido, Richard Howard, Timothy Donnelly, Eamon Grennan, and Mary Jo Salter. I owe a debt of gratitude to Carrie Bennett, Amaranth Borsuk, Jessica Bozek, Cheryl Clark Vermeulen, and Kevin McClellan for their generosity in reading and encouraging this book from start to finish, and to Danny Anderson and Joan Houlihan for their insightful comments on the manuscript. Also to my family and especially my husband and children, without whom I would have few poems to write.

IF A STORM

I

EVIDENCE

We come upon it —
the blown ribcage up-ended,

picked white as crocus tips in the long grass,
coil of vertebrae extended, skull nosing

the green suggestion of water
in the run-off ditch the elk was drinking from

when it fell. We can see our house
from here, over the last rise,

its collection of rocks and worry,
and beyond that, weather coming east,

skinning the gray jaw-lines of ridges.
Do we find these things — skull, roof,

the old ranch track down the ravine —
or are they in us like salt and nerve?

When we turn back
there is a grouse on the path,

a frenzy of dust and wing-beat
teasing us on as her four chicks start up

out of the brake to our left, hang uncertain,
then veer away.

THE WASPS

In late afternoon,
three small girls go out looking
for nests. They find one

belonging to the paper-makers —
its tiered gray egg grafted
to rotting board on the neighbor's porch.

If Beauty, hands joined in a circle.
If Luck, twice 'round with a hop.
From the low entrance, roar of mettle and wings.

Just as the blind woman feels boy or girl
through every stretched belly,
or the old man sees one hundred-year flood

from his ninety-ninth summer,
their mother hears screaming and knows
some world is over

as she puts on her wise face
behind the screen door: *blackberries for my hunters,*
tobacco-poultice for the sting.

Plague Column, Brno

Here, in a town we've chosen
for its white hotel room, sky-lit
by three cool rectangles of glass, we will recall

each paving block, so exactly plumbed
and placed, the thorough age of buildings
guyed to each other by tram wires,
and shut cathedrals quietly sunning.

Or, in Liberty Square, a Plague Column
rising from its base of imprisoned victims,
past corniced saints and lampposts,

to its haloed Virgin and Child
standing on a cow. Perhaps, years later,
town abbot Gregor Mendel would explain
such penance with science,

but this pillar, soothed round with height
against a fugue of iron balustrades and aerials,
holds no wiser knowledge than survival

as we pass it, returning each night to the square
bright bed where we lie down.

VINEYARD

In the thin, soured soil,
a perfect endurance: the grapes
steal alive from strangled vines
their tiny, sugary cathedrals.
Out of hardship, sweetness —
an ancient, learned fragility.

Deep among the rows,
we hear trucks on the road,
a dull bruise of sound beyond
the presses' shifting gravity.
Road to port, water, air, table, bed —
it's hum an alarm nearly forgotten
as we harvest (stooping slightly)
these gathering globes.

EVENING AUBADE

At 9 o'clock, the evening flights from JFK take off —
red eye to the Coast or overnight

to London, Dublin, Amsterdam, Madrid.
We see them from our bedroom window,

landing lights blinking as they ascend
toward clouds made momentarily

solid in their glow, and one that lifts
among them but never leaves — Venus

circling the runway. And here we are,
hard up against it once more.

By this I mean the body:
your arm across me, weighted with sleep,

already loosening its grip,
my shoulder parting us

like a ghost among the sheets. We've left
the curtains open to these nightly departures,

their thin jet whine a conch against the ear,
here in our dimming room.

UNDER THE SOUTHERN CROSS

— Sao Paolo, Brazil

Strange to this hemisphere, we
discover a white taxi

and lead it into topography, our atlas
disheveled with hesitations.

Not a mountain, but the road slopes up
into the sifted materials of a neighborhood —

humped and corrugated roofs
drop beards of balconies, and the leaky sigh

of bicycle brakes pass by
a man selling malarial liquor, gold-lit,

under an aluminum awning.
The November equator leans in,

and for a minute I think we could
misplace ourselves in distance here,

claim each other's last resort, keep driving.
At an intersection, two men deal cards

near an empty guard-hut —
no one watching or no one to watch for —

as the city stretches its constellations
toward some other horizon.

By Morning

You are asleep, the sheets
wound tight around
your feet, your body an insistence

of breathing. Helicopters
shudder overhead, as the city
presses in, passes on.

Yesterday, at the flower shop, I worried
about time — the gladiolas I'd chosen
closed tight with cold.

But after wine and fish,
we abandoned them and the dishes
to themselves. Now, rising for water,

I've caught them busy
with unfurling: a quiet marshalling
of color up the stalk —

pink, orange, yellow — awake
in this late summer
of electric light.

AFTER THE BADGER

Old glow off the tailing heaps,
the quarry dark behind, and a chatter
of loose boards on the creek bridge.

They've reopened the mine,
cyanide winnowing ore from the cuts.
Years ago, you saw a badger on this road,

and now we watch for her
each time we pass the gathering cabins
weighted by dusk. A kind of prospecting —

we've grown used to seeing,
from the corners of our eyes, the flash of bodies
leaving a scene. Tonight we drive farther,

to the river. We follow the crosshatch
of currents, a wide moon, and beneath,
only the sounds we've chosen to make.

PRAY, MONTANA

Lupine is the first to grow
after a fire. When settlers came here
they found it littering the soil,
bright as fresh-scrubbed laundry.
They got down from their wagons
to kneel for whatever was still there.

Everything is moving —
geysers sulfur-staining the trees,
the old burns roiling
under paintbrush and screwgrass,
the river coring inlets into sandbars,
sandbars into inlets.

You and I have been here before.
Tonight, on the porch
we drink whiskey and watch
lightning pass down the Yellowstone.
On a high slope across the valley,
a small fire begins.

IN THE CONSERVATORY

Follow me past the hanging jasmine
and the potted grapefruit tree fattening its suns

on the corner shelf. There are worse things,
maybe, than the orchid house —

its odd jewels clocked open for the crowds.
In the lagoon room, ferns thrum

a green archaeology, but what keeps here
knows how to stay warm.

Listen, six thousand years from now
they could unearth us,

preserved like those two spruces
at the bottom of Jenny Lake — twinned upright,

straight-grained and needle-perfect, enclosed
in all that water.

DEAR HURRICANE

Among red weeds off the Outer Banks,
I've sighted you —
your curl and call centering

in the low pressure of a Bermuda hour.
All the door frames list,
bewildered by trajectory,

and the bilge and batter
of your many scythes.
Careful, fledgling, the radar's up,

and the six o'clock news
just gave you a Christian name.
I've been wishing you so long

with my kerosene lamp,
each windowpane marking the spot —
have you had your fill already?

All this livid fall you've taught
the tidal islands to revolve,
as you bawl inland, inland.

At Low Tide

In town for a cousin's wedding,
we've borrowed a rowboat, wanting to trace

the canal, where reed beds fret the shipways
and Great Blues cast narrow shade

in the marsh lows. When we get close,
they crick their necks into lowercase Cs,

unleashing accordion wings to beat upwards
and away. Their matchstick legs dangle.

At the reception the night before,
the guests coupled off, awkward,

on the dance floor, the DJ culling us
by years married — 1, 5, 10 …

until the bride's grandparents waltzed 51 years alone.
In the boat, you face backward, rowing

as I navigate, calling out each stranded
high-water dock, their pilings gangly,

bleached bone by the sun.
Tomorrow, we'll fly home.

We'll hear, on arrival, of the accident —
the truck backing blind in the parking lot,

the grandmother dead as she stepped
from the curb.

But here in the canal, the heat reaches down,
slowing all to an eddy —

clank of oarlock, shush of wing,
suck of current against dock.

Instinct or pattern will blind us. Even now,
it is brighter as I remember it —

your hands resting the oars,
herons stalking minnows to the burgeoning shores.

HAWK WEATHER

The gliding seems an answer
to itself, as she inhabits air
above flat-roofed apartment blocks

and below the tracks of jet flight-paths,
describing wide concentric circles,
endless and precisely varying.

It's Saturday. At a nearby church,
limos honk the wedding march
each hour. The Red-tail's *keeer-r-r*

disturbs finches on fire-escape
feeders, and chimney swifts
to flight — impossible

to see a flying thing
and not think of a spirit rising —
but in all my weeks on watch

here by the kitchen window,
I've seen her brute arrow
dive just once, then come up empty.

THE INVENTION OF LIFE

And then we entered the year of dust
and lightning, where each day cracked
loud as a last word.

We moved in shifts
and slept when the other wasn't
looking. Everything fell from us —

geese losing their feathered vests
at the end of winter. *O world*,
we thought, *world in its infant cry*.

II

BALANCE

Learning to cross a log
over a fast stream
is a way to know grief:
the body following the mind
toward earth,
the eyes always ahead,
the arms outstretched,
the hands open —
weighted with air.

MISCARRIAGE

Little yolk, fly-speck, web
unworked, detail without name,
unlatch yourself from me, go.
In your small submersible,
your thousands of cells have stopped
beating. I felt their tappings
like braille on a quaking bog: a faint print,
then none. Go, almost thing,
the sundews have opened
their sticky pink mitts to catch
your brothers, and soon
the cranberries will float red
on the harvesting pond.

WOLF TREE

After many cautious hands,
after all needles and scans,
after the gurney,
after the anesthesiologist's blank magic,
after the emptying,

I came awake
like an old pasture tree waking,
crouched and knob-limbed,
among trunks straitened and unreluctant
for light, my familiar walls
lichen-pocked and seeded with ferns.

It was not quite fall,
and my leaves were about to turn.

OUT OF ETHER

It could be mist or blown sand,
this thing that takes
the light away — its fine tongue
lapping the last of it,
unbearing me
of one I would have borne.

When the world comes again,
I will puzzle it,
hinging and unhinging pictures,
reversing order as though I could
lift that gray muzzle,
unword its too-long answer.

In the yard, the trees lean
over the glass house
full of seeds and strivings —
even the doormat has birthed
feathery mushrooms — and the old jade
stretches its many crooked arms.

LUNA MOTH

On the coast of Maine, I have forgotten
yes for an answer. Last winter

the cottage faucet rusted open,
and now the tide will not leave

the bay, insistently nursing
the rocks and pilings.

I am exhausted by damp,
by what is no longer turning

inside me. Folded, quiet,
I walk the pine-needle courtyard —

no depth now,
only wind and drift. At night,

I stretch stilled wings
beneath the yellow porch light.

DEAR FLOOD

What world inhabits you?
In the bottom lands where you live,
skunk cabbage catacombs its roots

and even birds remember their gills.
When dog days batten us down,
you mourn through the valleys

on a raft of spare tires, spite,
and lawn ornaments, every lash
settling your score. I've seen you

bearing down fast in a lake
slapped wide open like a broken
hinge. What do you fathom

in those lost Midwestern seas,
fixed clear as Noah's stoic horizon? Shored
in my tin-cup town, I'm counting

lifeboats, until the harriers cry home
and your rivers withdraw,
wielding their deltas like rakes.

WAITING ROOM

The same year every year,
its moon-pocked exposure

mirror-written on the nerve.
Doctors' voices crowd the hall,

and each day I wake up counting:
minutes, months, degrees.

When is the hour when we begin
again, when the stranger we look for

arrives? Our view is a relief
of streets faceted with crowds

and flocks of small birds
guttering black-white-black-white

through the light.
Have we waited too long already?

Each night, I feel my slightest threads
unravel, relinquishing us both.

SEED

We found a milkweed pod in late fall
and set its pursed lip of smoke inside
on the hall shelf. March now,

we discover haloed seeds in every corner
looking to take root. This is what spring does:
splits and scatters us to the walls,

and we are sick with equinox.
Again, the gulls settle in the trees out back,
reminding us, even this far inland,

that there is harbor. They cry
for any bread at all, and we know this latitude —
that any hour could find itself in us

without notice. The eye holds what it can,
then releases it before the mind
has time to master: light, object, hand.

And still the giant spruce shades the house,
twisting its fingers toward us,
to drop its cones at our feet.

AT THE SEA WALL

We've left the old year
in the sag of trees before dark.
All the boats have been pulled ashore,
and ice has lifted the harbor buoys
like tops on a dusty mirror,
spinning so fast they're still.

At the wall, we look out
to where the tide does not enter
the narrow bay, the open water folding
and unfolding its black ridges
in the wind, while I stand dumb
as a long hallway, waiting
for any breath to tear through me —
stunned, animal, empty.

A Natural History

This summer, the icecaps balance
neat as thimble berries at the poles,

letting no drop spill, until lightning
girds the mountains, and the forests

give way. As we drive state roads,
we keep coming up against it —

the tindered stumps and charcoaled dirt
waiting for reincarnation,

something catching in the forest.
We walk miles, try dry streambeds for luck,

tracing their salt-licked curl
like dowsers whose sticks have gone deaf.

You carry the bucket, while I try to catch
the cool tremor of rescue, like that black bear cub

some rancher found treed up the ravine —
cat-sized, his paws scorched,

his tongue a blurred pink flag
of this place where the coming rains

are a skirt of smoke across the valley
that lifts into a sky burned through again.

FLIGHT

I

Too late, we found her:
a pinhole heart already slowing
its flutter through the ultrasound's static,
each beat slipping a further cog. O difference,
half-sister to chance, we watched for you
monthly, our landscape shortening
to horizon. We know now:
to begin is difficult, to stay, impossible.

Each evening, one grey owl flies out
and each morning returns to the creek aspen.
Walking the back fences at noon,
we find its mate caught against the barbs,
its skull all beak and socket,
its wing still feathered.

II
Its wing still feathered,
as though the breast — hollow bone
instrument — were waiting to breathe.
The field next to ours is grazed down,
and its cows watch us, hungry and shy.
Our acre is long with timothy and foxtail
and red cheat grass. At night,
the deer come to eat, their large dark shapes

followed by smaller ones.
Mornings we find their beds: oval bowls
pressed into the grass. We live in departure:
the mountain always ahead. Beyond our bodies
should be another, and beyond that —
this field can't be learned.

III
This field can't be learned,
not like the mountain, with its paths and forecast,
or the certain uncertainty of weather —
before a storm, the air tight with ignition,
the creeks worrying their banks.
We drive home by the river on washed roads
through red after-light, watching for the white pelicans
that fish from sandbars this time of year.

They have bred elsewhere
and shed their mating horns by now.
We've heard the reports, have memorized
the turns where rain can bring down rocks
on these roads, but repeat them to each other —
a means of naming what we pass by.

IV
A means of naming what we pass by —
this day, this night, this day.
From the porch, the land seems ordered,
the near hills yellow-green terraces of buffalo jumps,
the range rain-gray behind.
We find bitterroot by the driveway,
its bald flower tracing the curved slope
like a flood line.

The old gully that used to run here has gone dry,
starving the grove of aspen behind it.
Each summer, a few trees less.
Here, water is a migrating animal —
April melt, August rapids, October frost —
we meet again each new month.

V

Again, we meet each new month.
With time, I can hear what you've stopped saying —
Another one gone. We sleep
into late mornings and wake to find
the deer have broken into the garden,
eating the strawberries down to the roots.
Quicker than we are, they don't bother to wait
for the fruit to ripen. We abandon the fences

and drive to town, passing a doe
beside the highway, her fawn caught behind,
waiting to cross. The valley is smaller at this end
(enough to say everything has its limits),
the cliffs so close we might hang a curtain between them,
then draw it against the passing year.

VI

Draw a curtain against the passing year,
its voices catching and releasing
like low water across a stony creek bed.
We've listened long enough for doubt,
preferring the well's deliberate crank, sudden rain.
We've named ourselves immigrant,
put down the old expecting language of daughter,
of son — those dark cactus buds opening

to wax-pale flowers. Today, we see
a flock of sandhills feeding in the river meadow.
They clatter long, pointed bills to call their young
at our approach, but food is plentiful here,
the land wide enough for them to stay and watch,
to consider if warning is needed.

VII

If warning was needed
or had been offered. If the mountain,
shouldered in fir and penstemon,
was not always above. If any other life.
If sun, if a storm, if the waters raced high
every season, shielding all swimmers from capture.
If fireweed were as fierce as any blaze.
If another year, another day, another hour.

If the river ran south.
If you were not you, if I were not I.
If the body could be a bird,
righting itself in air, mating each wing-beat
to that frail fluttering within.
Too late, we found her.

III

WHAT IT WAS LIKE

In the beginning,
we didn't mind the dirt,
and when they gave us fire
we could stay warm,
which helped us to understand
kindness. We walked around
all day long picking things up:
shiny metal rocks, feathers,
what the animals had left for us.
They had been here longer,
but didn't seem to mind our arrival.
The mountains were always far away,
like forbidden ladders to the horizon.
We never learned how to swim.
When we looked up at night,
we waved to all the blinking gods
above us. We were sure they still
watched us, that if we became lonely
they would send someone else.

WHAT HER MOTHER SAID

When I found her, nettles had grown up
into her hair, and there were no gods left

in her eyes. Then winter crawled back
to its deeps, leaving my fields

to shake themselves out, warm and flat,
under scuttling clouds. But this was not

my doing. Don't speak to me
of myth — that black river, those six red seeds —

or sacrifice's ragged saw. You,
who have filled deserts with the drone

of mechanical birds, you have no quarter
here. No mother would be satisfied with half

her child. Even crocuses sour
in the brittle green of this spring.

IN A LOVE POEM FOR A RIVER

she is always leaving for the sea,
the sorrow of glaciers behind her.
Look how white she becomes,
hounding the rocks, drunk
with land. What can she carry?
Debris of an hour,
the clear tassel of months.
In a love poem for a river,
do not blame her when she loses
your boat in the roar of the sun —
the sky has crumpled into her,
and she cannot wait for you
to find her mouth.
Even the wharves lament —
clacking their teeth like stars —
as she wheels for the lighthouse.

ANNUNCIATION

— "Mérode Altarpiece," 1425-30, Robert Campin

Her whole life transfixed
by this moment: the miniature child
wielding his cross like a spear
toward her down the beam of light,

the angel waiting,
her teenage face still turned
(round cheeks, soft chin),
to her book. She doesn't see them,
nor do the burghers kneeling
outside her front door

recognize this intrusion yet,
while Joseph, busy with his drill
in his carpenter's shop next door,
puts out another mousetrap for display.

PHILOMELA IN AUGUST

Damage in the poppy beds:
the seed pods amputated
against harvest, blunted stalks
amid such blooming. Heat mounts
asphalt paths through the garden
and the air is slow.

What a girl he took.

On the ground, petals
curl like tongues, while beyond the wall
boats shuttle back and forth
under a tall bridge, tracing brief paths
through the water, then turning
to swallow their wakes.

DEAR EARTHQUAKE

In the sonogram of our dream
each wave unravels your hair like moths
seeding themselves through the woolens,

and all our lithic ages contract
to ink and sediment. Ore-throated
you divine our century: a leaded glass

poisoning itself loudly. What stirs you?
We take advantage of solidity,
derange our bedroom skyward, forget

old gods. Tell me,
when the many valves in your heart
begin to wake, cocking each chamber full,

will you remember our sacrifice:
that girl, wire-waisted, encased in flame?
Have you forgiven us yet?

MAGIC LANTERN

— Gojira, 1954, Ishirô Honda

Like a Salem girl drunk on ergot grass,
the monster collides through town,

and Tokyo replays her burning, frame
by frame. Nothing new happens,

then happens again — millennia
unreeling in a scaly rubber suit. It's dark

and the electric fences aren't working anymore.
We'll agree to hate this one thing.

Back at sea, Godzilla hovers: a cormorant,
neck fluting the waterline.

We lower our depth-charge
and the bay comes unhinged, swamping our boat

so that we barely notice his delicate
plastic skeleton settling on the rocks below.

FUSE

— Imperial Sugar Company, Port Wentworth, GA

From cane
juiced from wide sun
fields of South,
to kettles
boiling roundly,
to crystals,
in the narrows
of the refinery floor,
sugar dust collects,
whitely hissing
to ignition
in the silos' static
electric blast.

Then sweetness,
as the walls collapse,
sweetness
as men catch like torches
running from the pit,
sweetness,
enough to burn
a week of sky above
the near churchyard,
where, sweetness,
medics hang IVs
from pear trees
to nurse flayed workers
now laid out beneath.
(What is it we have made
from this earth?)

And, after,
in the air for months,
the scorch of caramel.

THE ROOM NEXT DOOR

— Basztowa St., Kraków, Poland

In the room next door,
a window looks out on an old stone gate.

In the room next door,
your mother's mother is sure — she remembers.

A market, Baltic and cool, and people walking
through a green afternoon,

in the room next door,
where soldiers are entering the city,

and the stories have all been planted — wired
along the wainscot in a fractious genealogy.

In the room next door,
a family sits down to dinner — wild mushrooms

and meat. They listen to the interrupted
trumpet call from the Cathedral

in the square. In the room next door,
someone else's father,

someone else's son. One voice says *purpose,*
another no longer speaks.

It smells faintly of ash in the room next door.
There are too many different words

for the pen on the empty table, a scrap of names,
the wood floor scarred by the broken-backed chair

in the room next door, where
we have been told, there was a room, once.

IV

WINTER FEEDING

— Celestún, Yucatan Peninsula

Our fishing-turned-tour boat stalls
and swerves toward the flamingos, hundreds

of heads lost in deliberate tilt and scoop,
each reed leg lifting, holding, falling

like calipers disrupted.
You translate for me as our guide explains

how the miniature pink shrimp of this lagoon
lend their color to the wintering flocks,

and we spot newcomers, whose day-old blush
will weekly spiral down each sloping neck

to their blunt bodies constantly disassembling
into flight. In the spring, each pair will deposit

a moon-white egg in the mud
beneath the mesh of trees along shore.

Always there is a before.
Would you name this ours?

There among the mangroves — roots knuckling
down to us, alive in either salt water or sweet.

And behind us the honking of those impossible birds
as we floated out on the inevitable current.

A Quickening

I strip choke-lines of poison ivy
from the trunk of our overgrown spruce
in the front yard — each new stem unearthing
a map of tendons from the needle-soft
ground beneath, their juice
raising bracelets of blister
between my gloves and shirt cuffs.

Pulling, I feel the *you* in me bear down,
readying — your moth fingers, frantic,
comb the dark. By this month,
each nail is in place, and we have counted
and recounted your bones
against despair. Now you must begin
to learn your own unrooting.

Leaving Alexandria

Those nine months
within your room,
blood hum the tonic to all song
you gathered in your floating
world, an everystory penned
in an astronomy of bones —
toe, elbow, ankle, thumb —
the physics of each curl and kick
lit by an encroaching drone
until that great rush
downward into cold,
invading thinness
and the first yellow
of an electric moon
reducing all within
its squall, each syllable,
fricative, vowel to mere
mew as you —
arms cocked, feet pedalling the air —
fought wordless for those walls
no longer there.

SUCH A THING AS LIGHT

From your infant window, I watch
the April limbs of the maple
move through the storm-lit sky.

You do not know *April* or *branch*
or *storm*. You know black
harrowing into white

the way you know milk
sharp in your throat
on its way to a place

that has asked for it,
that is unable to hold it,
and so must keep asking.

And this brightness you seek out
in every corner, every hour,
also cannot be held. Loss

will never again define itself
so simply: your eyelids, tendril veins
branching red across them, closing.

LEARNING TO SPEAK

February morning after a storm:
the slumped spruce a simple print
against a curdle of gray cloud,
each sound divided
from its source, so that we forget
icicle, car — hearing only *pop* and *stutter,*
their clatter nearing, then fading
like circling jets

or the cycle of months booming
and buzzing through your waking sleep.
Now, as your words take shape,
you hunker in them, senseless, hurling
each syllable at meaning like a wall,
and then no wall.

LIKE GIANTS

Their bodies airborne,
the big kids shout and fall

from the swings to a riptide
of elbows up the slide, legs spilling

across the wood plank bridge
to plunge over grass and then gone.

While you — stunned small
into your three year's self by these giants —

what do you sound like?
Today, the sky is a high blue tent,

but tomorrow it may collapse into worn,
gray wool. And sometimes the moon

wanders into the afternoon
as though it has forgotten its name.

If you spin around and then stop,
the ground escapes.

Someone is crying,
and you want to know why.

Also, where the birds are going
and how the deer lying next to the road last month

got there, and will it get up?
No. Not ever? No.

Each green leaf above, a question
you balance as you walk the perimeter wall,

one foot leading the other —
feeling for the edge.

A SPELL

As she waves the bright blue hose
over the baby's purple lips, giving him
the breaths he has not yet learned to take,
the nurse smiles at us: *to be expected.*

Expected: January drift and calm,
the routine earthquakes of passing plows,
and a black ice slope of sky the wind skitters down
from an immeasurable north.

Or, closer, the night shift trading its hours
for day, clockwork rounds of residents declaiming:
This is a 2223-gram product of a 34-year-old female.
Pregnancy complicated by ... The unseen Chief delivers

diagnosis: *prematurity, jaundice, apnea, all signs*
normal. And now his butterfly hands
expand, contract, dark-veined fingers reaching
toward the hiss of air cascading from above,

lid-flit and charcoal iris, and his mouth's soft O
receiving.

AFTER DAYLIGHT SAVINGS TIME

As if we could have owned this last light left
to us, jar it gleaming

with the winter pickles on the shelf above
the basement stairs. Now things begin

to happen more quickly — frost-thinned voices lance
the afternoon, last summer's boats lifted

to earth like broken toys wrapped and listing,
a collecting rattle of engine

and window frame as everything draws in —
each limb feeling for root, swept

of color or cover. And the body
of the child — small legs, chest,

hands — that loosens into a sleep
so deep he knows nothing but his own waking.

FLOOD TIDE

She yours? The stranger points
to the child's red raincoat tracing
the banks ahead of us, morning haze taking

the land from under her.
After ten year's drought,
the river has opened its flanks,

washing mineral
up cottonwood islands, pulling
at back yards, motels, and RV camps

uneasy behind sandbags along Rt. 89,
and sending its fingers into ditches
or beneath tarmac where,

eons ago, some ancestor lay down
and left her stony code.
Now, we stop on the bridge to watch

as pelicans flock — a clean white target
against the muddy waves.
And now she turns back to call us,

her voice lost in distances of sun
and the rapids between,
the small red arrow of her arm pointing

to the sudden birds as they lift
to twist and shift along the thermals —
rising, always rising.

Evening Song

Just as Venus sharpening
its red eye to a crescent proved
once more to Galileo
that we and Rome
aren't central to all there is
to know and be known
by, so you'll be my reflection —
your skull's soft curve
once fitted to my palm
now grown to turn
and face me. This
is certain, that there is no
certainty. The blue globe
of your eye wide now
takes in more tide
than ocean's light lets linger, so
we'll start here
to clothe ourselves in orbit —
each setting forth
a contract to return.

MOUNTAINS IN MONTANA

I

The freight line winds animal to the coast,
and this time of year the cows are up the mountains,
while we eat sky, dizzy as the day the land got up,
shook its weight north, and settled back down
sideways to the horizon. I almost remember it —
the blue, blue air, and we stood watching.

II

Seen from above:
small wood houses running into souvenir towns
where every calf escapes at the weekend rodeo
and the grain elevators along Main Street
lower the night. Where the wind fills us
with the taste of dry grass.

III

And that day we left the baby home and climbed —
do you remember? Hail loud as fall elk chasing us
back down though shale and underbrush.
Then rain-slick meadows — those ridges tangled
in light, the smell of copper in the air,
and her skin a current within us.

SALVAGE

We're past the north fork of Six Mile Creek,
where the trail levels and widens

whitely into an old mine road
rutted with grass and primrose but still

visible as wheel tracks, when we see it.
There, halfway down the ravine,

netted in brush and wedged
so that windshield, cracked headlamps,

and root-crimped grill point
towards us, as though caught escaping

the gasping water below, a 1940s pick-up
rests among the spruce trunks.

Junked, you say, but I want to look
further, peer through reflected branch

and sky to what slumps there:
some night-runner, scourer of slag-heaps,

debt-mired and ravenous
for luck, or whatever it is that pulls us,

the way, on summer nights,
my palm clings asleep to the bare slope

of your quiet shoulder blade.

LESSON

We enter the field through a rusted horse gate
to find the narrow trail through thickening
sagebrush and thistle, a few trees sentinel
along it leaking thin shade, or the memory
of shade, and then, so close we nearly tread on her,
a grouse hen racing up the path before us.
Flouncing her wings and stopping every few yards
to see that we are with her, she is dust-borne,
head bobbing in teasing panic. On and on she runs,
the precious nest far behind her by now, prey
to any other beast in the field, but not us.
Us, she is sure of. We will follow
her near-wounded hop and scuffle away
from what flickers behind, from what beats
unevenly against a shell that is home and halo and all,
follow as long as she will lead us.

DEAR FOG

Arrive unexpected on a day of sun:
we are dazzled, ocean-bound
coursing the narrows, or picnic-in-hand

halfway up the mountain. Give us
pines, wind-carved below the summit rock
or a single lighthouse. Promise hailstones,

bring only minor thunder. Allow singing,
if we must. Inhale the low countries
with their litter of harbors and insufficient

lighting. Erase fence-posts, oil-slicks,
garden-parties, all netting, but leave whistles,
engine chatter, and other glassy arguments.

No. Come only after a year without shade,
a century of prophecy and rain-dance,
after all indulgences are bartered and won.

Let us believe we deliver this ourselves.

ABOUT THE AUTHOR

Anna Ross's chapbook, *Hawk Weather,* won the New Women's Voices Prize from Finishing Line Press and the Jean Pedrick Chapbook Award from the New England Poetry Club. She has received fellowships from the Sewanee Writers' Conference, Grub Street Inc., Fishtrap, and the Massachusetts Cultural Council. Her work has twice been nominated for a Pushcart Prize. Her poetry and criticism has appeared in journals such as *The Paris Review, The New Republic, Southwest Review, Salamander, Barrow Street,* and *Boston Review.* She teaches at Stonehill College, where she is Poet in Residence, and is a contributing editor in poetry for *Guernica: A Magazine of Art & Politics.*